THE DIGITAL TIME

BOMB

THE HACKER WHO STOPPED A GLOBAL
CYBERATTACK

How One Developer's Sharp Instincts
Prevented the Biggest Hack in History

ERIC S. WESTMORLAND

TABLE OF CONTENT

INTRODUCTION

The digital age has brought us incredible advances, making life easier, faster, and more connected than ever before. But with every leap forward, a shadow lingers—a quiet, invisible danger that threatens to undo it all. In the blink of an eye, the things we take for granted can crumble, and the world we live in can come crashing down. This is not some far-fetched, apocalyptic scenario—this is a reality we came dangerously close to facing.

Imagine a world where every digital system you depend on—your bank account, your emails, your most sensitive data—is vulnerable to attack. Picture a hacker, a phantom in the vast, intricate web of the internet, silently pulling the strings, on the verge of launching a global cyberattack that could shatter economies, cripple governments, and throw societies into chaos.

This wasn't a theoretical disaster. It almost happened. The culprit? A small, seemingly insignificant piece of code, expertly hidden in the underbelly of an open-source software tool, which powers the servers of governments, hospitals, and businesses alike. It was the kind of backdoor that no one saw coming—until one keen developer noticed a strange, almost imperceptible glitch.

What followed was nothing short of heroic. One person, a single developer with a sharp eye, would stand between this silent threat and a global catastrophe. The events that unfolded in the coming days would expose the vulnerabilities of our digital infrastructure and reveal just how close we were to an unprecedented crisis.

This is the untold story of how a hacker almost brought the internet to its knees, and how one developer—Andres— stepped into the breach, saving not just millions of servers but the entire digital world.

As the world holds its breath, and the hackers behind this attack continue to lurk in the shadows, the question remains: what will it take to stop the next time bomb from detonating?

The digital world may feel safe, but make no mistake—nothing is ever truly secure.

CHAPTER 1

The Calm Before the Storm

The morning started like any other for Andres. As a software developer, his routine was predictable: booting up his system, launching a few tests, and reviewing some code. It was part of the ebb and flow of the workday, a never-ending cycle of debugging, tweaking, and refining. But on this particular day, something felt... off.

As he ran his usual tests, Andres noticed a subtle anomaly—a peak in the CPU load. It wasn't enough to be alarming, not at first glance. His system was working harder than usual, but not to the extent that it would crash or cause any major issues. In fact, most people would have dismissed it as a minor glitch, just another one of those small hiccups that comes with the territory of managing complex systems. But Andres wasn't most people. His mind was sharp, and he had an eye for patterns that others might overlook.

He paused, studying the graph on his screen. The anomaly seemed insignificant, just a blip in the otherwise steady rhythm of his system's performance. Still, he felt an uneasy tug at the back of his mind. Something wasn't right. It wasn't about the magnitude of the issue—it was about the fact that it didn't fit the usual patterns of behavior he'd come to expect. The data didn't make sense.

Andres was used to dealing with bugs, errors, and performance glitches, but this was different. It was almost like the system was hiding something—something that was just below the surface, waiting to reveal itself. A few more tests confirmed his suspicion: the load wasn't a random spike, and it wasn't just an error. It was a symptom of something deeper. But what?

He dove deeper into the data, trying to understand why this particular anomaly was occurring. As he examined the code and tracked down the source of the issue, it became clear: this wasn't just a technical glitch. What he was looking at was a subtle, carefully hidden backdoor—one that had been planted into the system long before he ever noticed it.

What Andres didn't know was that this seemingly harmless issue was the first sign of something much more sinister. This backdoor wasn't a mere bug; it was the entry point to a cyberattack so sophisticated that it could have compromised entire networks. But at this point, all Andres could see was a strange anomaly—a mystery that needed solving. He had no idea that this small discovery would soon lead him to the brink of a global crisis.

In the world of software development, anomalies are often ignored or brushed aside. Most of the time, they turn out to be nothing more than harmless bugs. But this time, Andres's instincts told him something was different. What started as a routine test was about to unravel into one of the most dangerous cybersecurity threats the world had ever seen. And all it took was a developer's sharp eye, a quick decision, and the quiet tension of a system struggling to keep its secrets hidden.

What Andres didn't know yet was that he had just stumbled upon a ticking time bomb. A digital time bomb that, if left undetected, could have shattered the very systems that run our world.

CHAPTER 2

The World of Open-Source Software

The digital world we live in today is built on a delicate foundation—one that rests on the shoulders of thousands of open-source projects. Open-source software is the unsung hero of the internet, quietly powering everything from small websites to massive global infrastructures. It's the very backbone of the modern tech world, running on the systems of governments, businesses, hospitals, and universities alike. Without open-source software, our digital lives would look drastically different, and much less efficient.

Open-source software, at its core, is software whose source code is made available to the public. Anyone with the skills and knowledge can look at the code, suggest improvements, and even contribute to the development of the software itself. It's a collaborative approach that has transformed the way we think about software development. Rather than being controlled by a single company or entity, open-source projects are typically managed by a community of developers—

enthusiasts, professionals, and volunteers—who work together to improve the software.

This model has given birth to some of the most widely used software in the world, including the Linux operating system, Apache web server, and, of course, XZ utils—a data compression tool embedded in countless Linux systems. For those who may not be familiar, XZ utils compresses and packages data so it can be transferred and stored more efficiently, much like a ZIP file on your computer. It's a small cog in a much larger machine, but its significance cannot be overstated. This single tool is found in the majority of Linux distributions, which power much of the internet's infrastructure.

At the helm of many open-source projects, like XZ utils, are maintainers—dedicated individuals responsible for overseeing the project's development. Lassa Colin, for example, had been the maintainer of XZ utils for over a decade. Colin was not just a contributor; he was the lifeblood of the project. As the maintainer, it was his job to ensure that the software remained functional, secure, and up-to-date. He reviewed and approved contributions, decided which changes would be incorporated into the project, and kept an eye on any potential issues that might arise.

But being a maintainer wasn't always easy. Colin, like many others in his position, was juggling this responsibility alongside other commitments in his personal and professional life. For years, he had single-handedly managed the project, but over time, the weight of it all started to take its toll. As XZ utils became more integral to the functioning of Linux distributions, the demands on Colin's time and attention grew exponentially. The project was no longer a simple hobby—it was a massive undertaking, and Colin found himself stretched thin, struggling to keep up with the flood of updates and requests coming his way.

This is where the beauty of open-source software comes into play. Unlike proprietary software, which is tightly controlled by a single company or team, open-source projects allow anyone with the necessary expertise to contribute. Anyone who sees a problem, has an idea for an improvement, or simply wants to help can submit changes to the project. This collaborative approach has made open-source software not only incredibly powerful but also remarkably flexible. The collective knowledge and expertise of thousands of contributors allow the software to grow and evolve at an astonishing pace.

However, this openness comes with a catch. While open-source projects are a testament to the power of collaboration, they also present significant risks. The same openness that allows anyone to contribute can also be exploited. A single malicious actor, like a hacker, can slip a dangerous piece of code into an open-source project without anyone noticing. The process of reviewing contributions, though thorough, is ultimately dependent on the maintainers—and if a maintainer is overwhelmed or distracted, even the smallest error can have catastrophic consequences.

This was the problem that would soon unfold with XZ utils. As Colin struggled to manage the growing demands of the project, he found himself leaning more and more on external contributors. And that's when Tan appeared. Seemingly harmless at first, Tan's contributions quickly became more significant, until she was eventually promoted to co-maintainer. What started as innocent collaboration would soon take a dark turn.

The open-source ecosystem, for all its innovation and power, is not without its flaws. While the collective effort behind these projects is a marvel, the risks of relying on volunteers and contributors who may not always have the necessary security training are ever-present. This delicate balance between openness and security would soon be tested in ways no one could have predicted.

And it all started with one unassuming tool—XZ utils.

CHAPTER 3

Enter Tan

Tan's arrival into the world of XZ utils was quiet, almost unnoticed. A new contributor among many, Tan first appeared in the project's repository with small, innocuous changes—bug fixes, minor improvements, and some tweaks to the code that were typical of any open-source contributor. At the time, nothing about her stood out as unusual. She was just another developer, offering her help to make XZ utils better, just as so many others had done before her.

But what seemed like routine participation was, in reality, the beginning of a calculated journey. Tan didn't rush in with grand gestures or overwhelming contributions. Instead, she adopted a patient, methodical approach—one that would eventually win her the trust of the XZ utils community. Every contribution was small, precise, and always with a tone of helpfulness. She asked thoughtful questions, suggested improvements, and accepted feedback graciously. In an open-source community, where collaboration and trust are essential, this approach worked wonders. Tan quickly became a familiar and respected name, a contributor who seemed genuinely dedicated to the improvement of the software.

Over the next year, Tan's involvement grew. She didn't just fix minor bugs or add trivial features; she started taking on more substantial changes. Each of her updates was well-documented, and her interactions with other contributors were always polite and professional. She was always quick to praise the efforts of others, a strategy that reinforced the sense of community and collaboration. Slowly but surely, Tan started to become a pillar of the project. Her growing presence wasn't noticed by many, but for those who paid attention, it was clear that Tan was no longer just an occasional contributor. She was becoming indispensable.

It wasn't long before Lassa Colin, the longtime maintainer of XZ utils, began to feel the pressure of his own responsibilities. The project had grown significantly over the years, and with it came a flood of requests and updates that needed his attention. Colin had always been the project's main gatekeeper, deciding which contributions would be integrated into the codebase. But as time wore on, his ability to keep up with the demands of XZ utils became more strained. Colin had never expected the project to grow to the scale it had, and his responsibilities as a maintainer were weighing heavily on him.

He started to fall behind, and that's where Tan saw her opportunity.

Tan had become more than just a contributor—she had become an ally, a reliable presence in the community. Colin, now burdened by his workload, began to lean on Tan more and more. She helped manage incoming contributions, reviewed code changes, and handled tasks that were becoming increasingly overwhelming for Colin. At first, it seemed harmless—a natural progression in the life of any project where the maintainers need help to stay afloat. Tan's increasing involvement seemed to be a natural solution to Colin's struggles.

But what no one realized was that Tan wasn't just helping to ease Colin's burden; she was slowly positioning herself to take control of the project. As she became more involved, her influence within the community grew. Her suggestions carried weight, and her actions seemed to shape the future of XZ utils in subtle but significant ways. It wasn't long before Tan was promoted to co-maintainer—a position that gave her the power to approve and merge code changes without needing to go through Colin's approval.

Colin, exhausted and overwhelmed, welcomed the help. He was glad to have someone he could trust to take on more of the responsibilities. After all, Tan had been a helpful and competent contributor, and it seemed only logical that she should take on more authority within the project. He even started to confide in Tan, expressing his frustrations and worries about the project's future. For a while, everything seemed to be going smoothly. But what Colin didn't realize was that the balance of power had shifted. Tan, now in control of the project, held the keys to its future, and with it, the potential to change everything.

This wasn't just about helping maintain an open-source project; this was a long con—a slow, deliberate process of gaining trust, assuming control, and positioning herself at the helm of one of the most critical pieces of open-source infrastructure in the world. Tan had successfully ingrained herself in the community, and her presence was now so deeply woven into the fabric of XZ utils that no one suspected a thing. What began as a small, seemingly innocent contribution had turned into a takeover of the project.

In the end, it was a brilliant strategy—a quiet infiltration into the heart of a trusted community, all while maintaining the appearance of being just another passionate developer. But as Tan took the reins, she wasn't just controlling code anymore. She was controlling access to one of the most powerful tools in the digital world—a tool that would soon become the gateway for a devastating cyberattack.

CHAPTER 4

The Hidden Backdoor

For most people, the intricacies of code and software development remain invisible. The complex algorithms, the minute details that make digital systems run smoothly, are often taken for granted. But in the dark corners of the code, there are dangers—hidden threats that can compromise the entire system. This was the case with XZ utils, a tool that millions of servers depended on. A tool that, unbeknownst to its users, contained a secret waiting to be discovered.

Tan, now in control of the XZ utils project, had access to the codebase. Over time, she began to subtly alter its functions, injecting a malicious backdoor that would remain nearly invisible to anyone who wasn't actively searching for it. This wasn't the kind of error that could be spotted easily; it wasn't a bug or a glaring vulnerability. No, this backdoor was far more insidious—it was hidden deep within the code, disguised to blend in with the normal functions of the software.

The backdoor was expertly inserted, crafted to appear as a minor adjustment or an inconsequential patch. On the surface, everything seemed perfectly normal. The code was clean, the updates appeared to be improvements or fixes, and there was nothing to indicate that anything was amiss. This was the genius of Tan's manipulation: she knew exactly how to disguise the backdoor in a way that wouldn't raise suspicion. It was so well hidden that even the most experienced developers couldn't detect it in routine reviews.

But this wasn't an ordinary vulnerability. It was a backdoor that, when activated, would allow remote access to any system running XZ utils. A hidden passageway, waiting for the right moment to be exploited. The backdoor was inserted in a way that ensured it wouldn't show up in basic security scans or audits. To the casual observer, the code looked flawless. It wasn't until Andres, running tests on an unstable version of Linux, noticed something strange that the backdoor was even uncovered. It was a flaw in the system's performance—a seemingly minor glitch that would eventually lead to the discovery of the backdoor.

The intricacies of how the backdoor operated were as complex as they were dangerous. The code was carefully crafted to trigger only under specific conditions, and its effects were subtle. It didn't crash the system, nor did it cause any immediate signs of distress. Instead, it lay dormant, quietly waiting for a chance to be activated. It was designed to operate under the radar, never calling attention to itself, while quietly opening a door for remote access from anyone who knew how to exploit it.

One of the most critical aspects of this backdoor was its connection to SSH, or Secure Shell. SSH is a widely used protocol that allows users to remotely access and control systems, typically on Linux servers. It's a secure method of communication, encrypted to protect sensitive data. But in this case, the backdoor in XZ utils was intricately tied to SSH, allowing an attacker to access a machine through an entirely legitimate channel. The vulnerability wasn't in SSH itself; rather, it was in the way that XZ utils interacted with SSH.

The backdoor was activated when certain XZ functions were called by SSH. The malicious code was cleverly embedded into these functions, so when a user initiated an SSH session, the backdoor would spring to life, giving the attacker remote access to the system. This connection between XZ utils and SSH was crucial, as it allowed the attacker to bypass the usual security measures and gain full control over a machine without raising any alarms. It was a masterstroke of design— hidden in plain sight, leveraging the trust and reliability of SSH to carry out its sinister purpose.

This wasn't just a minor flaw; this was a serious vulnerability that posed a massive threat to systems around the world. Had it gone unnoticed, the backdoor could have spread like wildfire, infecting servers, government systems, and businesses across the globe. The attacker would have gained unrestricted access to millions of machines, with the potential to cause untold damage.

The danger wasn't just in the backdoor itself, but in how it was integrated into a trusted, widely used system. It was invisible yet powerful, a silent threat waiting to be unleashed. And the fact that it had been hidden so carefully—camouflaged in the very fabric of the software—meant that it would have been incredibly difficult to detect and neutralize without a sharp eye. It was only because Andres noticed the performance anomaly and dug deeper that the backdoor was exposed.

This hidden backdoor, expertly crafted and concealed, was a ticking time bomb in the world of digital security. Its connection to SSH made it especially dangerous, as it exploited an already trusted and secure protocol to gain access to sensitive systems. In the hands of the wrong person, it could have led to a global catastrophe—one that could have crippled entire infrastructures and compromised the very systems that keep our world running. And yet, it was almost missed. Almost.

CHAPTER 5

Andres's Discovery

Andres had always prided himself on his attention to detail. It was this skill, more than any other, that made him a valuable developer at Microsoft. So, when he began testing the unstable Sid version of Linux—a testing ground for new code—he wasn't just doing his job. He was constantly alert, searching for anything that seemed even remotely out of place. That's when he noticed the first red flag.

The performance drop was subtle at first, but it was there. SSH, the secure protocol used to remotely access Linux machines, was suddenly consuming an unusually high amount of resources. Most people wouldn't have noticed it—half a second of lag here and there might be dismissed as nothing more than a routine hiccup. But Andres wasn't like most people. His experience had taught him that small anomalies like this could often signal something much deeper. And what he found next made his blood run cold.

It wasn't just a minor delay or a glitch. As he dug into the data, he noticed that the system's performance was being affected in ways that didn't make sense. There was a consistent drop in response times, and the system was draining more CPU resources than it should have. Andres traced the issue back to XZ utils, the widely-used compression tool that was embedded in the Sid version of Linux.

At first, he thought it might be a bug or some minor error in the code. But the deeper he dug, the more suspicious the situation became. Something wasn't right—this wasn't just a random bug. It was as if the system was working harder than it should, and yet there was no logical explanation for the increased load. It didn't take long for Andres to realize that what he was looking at wasn't a glitch. This wasn't a simple coding error. It was something far more dangerous.

Andres's investigation led him to uncover something that sent a chill down his spine. Hidden deep within XZ utils was a piece of malicious code—a backdoor that allowed for remote access to the system. It was a vulnerability so carefully concealed that no one had detected it before. The code was subtle, integrated seamlessly into the tool's functions, making it nearly impossible to spot. But Andres wasn't deterred. He followed the trail of breadcrumbs, digging deeper into the software until he found the hidden code.

What he discovered was nothing short of terrifying. This backdoor, if left unchecked, could give an attacker full control over any system running XZ utils. It was a well-crafted exploit, designed to trigger only under specific conditions, and it relied on SSH to provide unauthorized access. The fact that the exploit was buried in a trusted, widely-used tool like XZ utils made it all the more dangerous. It was a vulnerability that could spread quickly and quietly, compromising entire networks without raising any alarms.

Andres knew the gravity of what he had found. He couldn't keep this discovery to himself—not when the consequences of ignoring it could be so catastrophic. Without hesitation, he took immediate action. First, he reached out to the Debian security team, informing them of the issue and providing all the necessary details about the backdoor he had uncovered. The urgency of his message was clear—this wasn't just another bug fix; this was a potential global security threat. He couldn't afford to wait for the problem to spread.

But even after reporting the issue to the security team, Andres knew that the threat couldn't be contained by private communications alone. The world needed to know. So, he made the bold decision to go public. He published a post on Mastodon, a decentralized social platform, explaining the nature of the vulnerability and warning others about the backdoor hidden in XZ utils. He laid out the details of his findings, describing how the exploit worked and the potential damage it could cause.

In doing so, Andres didn't just raise awareness of the issue; he set in motion a series of events that would spark a global response. The world of cybersecurity, which had been largely unaware of the threat, now had a clear understanding of the danger they were facing. The Debian security team moved quickly, issuing alerts and coordinating with other organizations to patch the vulnerability before it could be exploited on a larger scale. The race against time had begun, and thanks to Andres's vigilance, the digital world was finally aware of the ticking time bomb that had been quietly embedded in their systems.

What Andres had done was nothing short of heroic. His decision to report the issue and make it public saved countless systems from being compromised. Had he not noticed the performance drops, had he not followed the trail of evidence, the backdoor could have remained undetected—spreading across networks, opening the door for a global cyberattack that could have devastated critical infrastructure.

In the end, it was Andres's quick thinking and commitment to uncovering the truth that averted a disaster. His discovery was a wake-up call to the digital world, a reminder of how fragile our systems really are and how easily a hidden threat could bring everything to a standstill. But for now, thanks to Andres's immediate action, the digital world had narrowly escaped a catastrophe.

CHAPTER 6

The Cyberattack Unraveled

The moment Andres went public with his discovery, the digital world was thrown into chaos. His post on Mastodon sent shockwaves through the cybersecurity community, alerting experts, developers, and security teams to the imminent danger that had been lurking in the system. What had seemed like a routine bug report suddenly became a full-scale emergency. The realization set in quickly: this wasn't just an isolated issue. This backdoor could have been exploited at any moment, unleashing a cyberattack of unprecedented scale.

The panic was palpable. Within hours of Andres's public revelation, cybersecurity teams around the world scrambled into action. The news spread like wildfire, as other developers, system administrators, and security professionals began to realize just how close they had come to disaster. This wasn't just a minor bug or an obscure vulnerability; this was a ticking time bomb, one that could have torn through the very fabric of the digital world. For many, the magnitude of the threat had only just become clear.

In the early hours following the revelation, the race to neutralize the threat was on. The Debian security team, which had been informed by Andres earlier, worked tirelessly to patch the vulnerability in XZ utils. They weren't alone in their efforts—security experts from around the world jumped into action, coordinating with other open-source projects to ensure that the backdoor didn't spread any further. Every developer, every IT specialist, and every cybersecurity expert was now focused on one goal: to prevent this backdoor from being exploited before it was too late.

The problem was urgent. Systems running XZ utils, an essential piece of open-source software, were widespread—every major Linux distribution, from the ones running on personal computers to those controlling critical infrastructure, could potentially be affected. The backdoor had been cleverly hidden within a trusted tool, one that was already in use by millions of servers around the world. If the malicious code had been activated, it would have been a disaster of global proportions.

Security patches were rushed into production, and software updates were sent out across the world, but there was no guarantee that every vulnerable system would be updated in time. The digital infrastructure of entire governments, corporations, and service providers was at risk. The cybersecurity community worked in overdrive, monitoring networks for any signs of exploitation, making sure to close the backdoor as quickly as possible. The clock was ticking, and every second counted.

Had the backdoor been activated, the consequences would have been catastrophic. At the most basic level, the attackers could have gained unauthorized access to millions of systems, allowing them to steal sensitive data, deploy malicious software, or even completely shut down critical services. Imagine the chaos that would have ensued: hospitals' systems compromised, government communications intercepted, financial institutions brought to their knees. The potential damage was unimaginable.

But the threat didn't stop there. Once in control of a system, the attackers could have spread malware across networks, infecting other machines and creating a ripple effect that would have been felt globally. A single backdoor could have been the gateway to a massive, coordinated cyberattack, one that could have crippled the world's digital infrastructure. The attackers could have disrupted supply chains, interrupted communication systems, and triggered widespread panic as entire cities were cut off from their vital services. The very systems that society relies on for safety, security, and communication were vulnerable—and without a swift response, they would have been brought to their knees.

It was more than just a potential breach of data; it was the possibility of a systemic collapse. Critical services could have been wiped out, leaving the world's most vulnerable systems exposed and defenseless. What's worse, no one could have predicted just how far the attack might have gone. Given the scale and sophistication of the threat, the attackers could have infiltrated national security systems or global networks, spreading chaos on an unimaginable scale.

But thanks to Andres's quick action—his attention to detail, his instinct to dig deeper, and his decision to go public—the disaster was averted. The backdoor was sealed, the vulnerability patched, and the digital world narrowly escaped what could have been one of the largest cyberattacks in history. The cybersecurity community breathed a collective sigh of relief, but the lessons learned from this close call were invaluable.

The incident was a stark reminder of the fragility of our digital systems and the importance of vigilance in the face of ever-evolving threats. Had Andres not acted when he did, the story could have been far different. This time, the digital world had dodged a bullet—but the question lingered: how many more time bombs were waiting to go off? And how long could the world continue to rely on open-source software without better safeguards to protect it from such insidious threats?

CHAPTER 7

Theories Behind the Attack

As Andres reflected on the events that had just unfolded, a troubling thought gnawed at him: Was Tan truly acting alone? The sophistication of the attack and the careful planning behind it suggested something far more intricate than a lone developer taking advantage of an open-source project. Andres's instincts told him that this was no simple case of an individual acting out of self-interest. There was something larger at play, something more methodical, and it raised the chilling possibility that Tan was merely a pawn in a much broader, state-sponsored cyberattack.

At first glance, Tan had seemed like just another dedicated open-source contributor—a well-meaning developer who made improvements to the project and helped push the software forward. But as Andres delved deeper into the timeline of events, it became clear that Tan's rise to prominence within the project wasn't a mere coincidence. She had carefully infiltrated the XZ utils community, gained trust, and maneuvered herself into a position of influence. But it wasn't just her actions that raised suspicion—it was the larger network of contributors who seemed to support her rise.

Andres's suspicions began to mount as he connected the dots between Tan and other contributors who had been heavily involved in the project. One of the key figures in this web of influence was Jansen, a contributor who had pushed for an update to XZ utils that included the very backdoor that Andres had discovered. Jansen, like Tan, had been part of the broader community, but his involvement in the update seemed more than coincidental. Along with others like Koran and Mizo, Jansen had been instrumental in advocating for the integration of the malicious code into the project. Together, they had worked to push the update through the system, using their collective influence to silence any concerns and speed up the approval process.

What was most striking about their involvement was how seamlessly they had worked together to manipulate the project's trajectory. Each of them played a role in the execution of the attack, but none of them seemed to be acting independently. Their coordinated efforts hinted at a deeper, more calculated plan—one that suggested they were operating as part of a larger agenda. And for Andres, the pieces started to fall into place: this wasn't just about a rogue developer looking to exploit a popular open-source tool. It was the work of a group that was deliberately infiltrating open-source projects, laying the groundwork for a global cyberattack. The question was no longer "Who is Tan?" but "Who is behind Tan?"

The manipulation didn't stop with the contributors. It was clear that social engineering was a key element of this attack. The backdoor, once introduced into the project, relied not only on technical skill but also on psychological manipulation. Social engineering—the practice of manipulating people into revealing confidential information or performing certain actions—was at play here. Tan had expertly ingrained herself within the community, building relationships, earning trust, and even appealing to the frustrations of other contributors who felt that the project was being neglected. It was a classic example of social engineering: manipulating human behavior to gain access to something valuable, in this case, the ability to push a malicious update through an open-source project.

Tan's involvement in the XZ utils project was a textbook case of how social engineering can infiltrate even the most secure systems. By gradually working her way up the ranks, she was able to create the perfect storm—a community of developers who trusted her, a tool that millions relied on, and a backdoor that would remain hidden in plain sight until it was too late. But the tactics didn't stop there. The contributors who supported Tan's updates, like Jansen, Koran, and Mizo, weren't just acting out of a shared vision for the software. They were, knowingly or unknowingly, part of a broader plan that was designed to manipulate and deceive the community into accepting a dangerous, malicious code update.

For Andres, the discovery of this network of influence was both shocking and enlightening. It revealed how easy it was to manipulate the open-source ecosystem—an environment built on trust and collaboration—into a tool for global sabotage. The attack had been as much about exploiting human psychology as it had been about exploiting the software itself. Tan and her accomplices understood this dynamic all too well. They used their knowledge of the community's structure, its values, and its vulnerabilities to execute a plan that would have devastated the digital world.

As Andres continued to investigate, the evidence pointed more and more to the possibility of a state-sponsored attack. The sophisticated nature of the backdoor, the careful orchestration of contributors, and the deliberate manipulation of the open-source process all pointed to a level of coordination that was far beyond the scope of individual hackers or rogue developers. Andres suspected that Tan, Jansen, Koran, and Mizo weren't just motivated by personal gain—they were part of something much larger. The timing of their involvement, the precision of the attack, and the scale of the operation all indicated that they were working on behalf of a foreign government, possibly one with the resources and expertise to carry out such a sophisticated infiltration.

Theories about the true nature of the attack circulated in the cybersecurity community. Some believed it was the work of a hacker group, while others suspected the involvement of state-sponsored hackers from Russia or China—nations with a known history of using cyberattacks as a tool for geopolitical influence. But regardless of the true identity of the attackers, one thing was certain: the attack was no accident. It was the result of a highly orchestrated plan, executed with precision and patience, and it was only thanks to Andres's discovery that the world was given a glimpse into the dangerous reality of digital warfare.

What had started as a simple open-source contribution had quickly spiraled into a full-scale conspiracy—one that exposed the vulnerabilities in the very systems that powered our connected world. And as Andres pieced together the theories behind the attack, he couldn't shake the chilling thought: what other open-source projects had been targeted in the same way? How many more digital time bombs were quietly waiting to explode?

CHAPTER 8

Who Was Tan?

As the investigation into the attack deepened, one question lingered in the air: Who was Tan? To the community of developers and maintainers, Tan had been just another contributor—a name that had gradually become familiar but never quite stood out. Yet, now that the full scale of the cyberattack was becoming clear, the mystery surrounding Tan's true identity grew more ominous. Was Tan truly who she claimed to be, or had she been hiding something much darker all along?

The truth was, very little was known about Tan. She had appeared in the open-source community with no fanfare, gradually contributing to various projects, including XZ utils, where she made a name for herself by fixing bugs and suggesting improvements. Her approach was measured, professional, and seemingly harmless. But as Andres and other security experts began to dig deeper into the timeline of her contributions, a pattern began to emerge—one that raised suspicions about her true intentions.

One of the most intriguing aspects of Tan's online presence was the lack of concrete information about her. While she had contributed extensively to XZ utils, and her interactions with other developers were always cordial and respectful, there was little to no personal information available. No public social media accounts, no online presence outside of the GitHub repository, and no mention of her real-world identity. For someone who had gained such prominence within the open-source community, this absence of personal details stood out. It wasn't unusual for developers to keep their personal lives private, but Tan's complete lack of traceable history raised alarms.

Then came the revelation that would shake the entire investigation: the possibility that Tan had been deliberately hiding her true identity. Analysts who had been looking into Tan's online activity noticed something strange in the timestamps of her contributions. While the majority of her updates came from a timezone consistent with East Asia, there were several instances where her contributions appeared to come from different time zones, specifically those typical of Eastern Europe. The discrepancies were small, almost imperceptible, but they were there. It seemed as though Tan was manipulating the time zone settings on her account to create a false trail, one that would mask her true location and intentions.

The analysts dug deeper, trying to piece together the puzzle of Tan's online movements. They discovered that, while Tan had seemingly worked through major Chinese holidays—suggesting she might be based in China—there were periods when her contributions were made during regular business hours in Eastern Europe. This discrepancy, while subtle, suggested that Tan may have been faking her location, using different time zones to obscure her true origins. It was a clever tactic, one that would make it far more difficult for anyone to trace her movements or make any assumptions about her background.

At first, the time zone deception seemed like a small detail, something that could be easily dismissed as an oversight. But as experts continued to investigate, it became clear that it was a deliberate attempt to mislead. Why would Tan, a seemingly harmless open-source contributor, go to such lengths to hide her true location? What was she trying to conceal? These questions lingered in the minds of investigators as they pushed forward with their efforts to uncover the truth.

The more Andres and the cybersecurity experts looked into Tan's involvement, the more they began to suspect that she was not just a lone actor in this scheme. In fact, the patterns in her online behavior and her use of time zone manipulation pointed toward the possibility of a much larger operation. Many in the cybersecurity community began to theorize that Tan's actions were not just the result of personal ambition, but rather part of a coordinated effort by a state-sponsored hacking group. The theories began to point toward one group in particular: APT29, also known as Cozy Bear, a notorious Russian hacker collective with a history of sophisticated cyberattacks.

APT29 had been responsible for some of the most high-profile cyber espionage campaigns in recent history. Their attacks had targeted governments, corporations, and critical infrastructure, often using highly sophisticated techniques to infiltrate systems and steal sensitive information. The group was known for its patience and meticulous planning, characteristics that seemed to align perfectly with Tan's slow and careful infiltration of the XZ utils project.

Experts began to draw connections between Tan's behavior and the known tactics of APT29. The time zone manipulation, the calculated nature of her contributions, and the eventual takeover of the XZ utils project all resembled the techniques employed by Cozy Bear. They were known for their ability to infiltrate open-source projects and other public-facing platforms, using these opportunities to plant malicious code that could be exploited later. The backdoor inserted into XZ utils, with its subtle, almost undetectable design, was eerily similar to the type of attack APT29 was known for.

While no definitive evidence could link Tan directly to APT29, the similarities were too striking to ignore. Cybersecurity experts speculated that Tan might have been a "sleeper agent" placed within the open-source community to lay the groundwork for a larger cyberattack. The idea that a state-sponsored group could infiltrate the open-source ecosystem in such a sophisticated way was both chilling and eye-opening. It underscored the vulnerability of the digital world and the lengths to which adversaries would go to exploit these weaknesses.

Tan's true identity may never be fully known, and the extent of her involvement in the attack may remain a mystery. But one thing was clear: the attack was far from the work of a single rogue developer. It was part of a larger, well-coordinated effort, possibly backed by a state-sponsored group with the resources and expertise to carry out such a complex and dangerous attack. The mystery of Tan—and the possibility that she was part of something much bigger—had added a new layer of complexity to the already terrifying events that had unfolded.

CHAPTER 9

Lessons Learned from the Attack

The attack on XZ utils was a wake-up call for the entire digital world, a stark reminder that the very systems we rely on every day are not as secure as we think. Open-source software, while a marvel of collaboration and innovation, is inherently vulnerable. The attack that nearly compromised millions of servers exposed the fragility of a system built on trust, volunteerism, and community-driven development. It was a vulnerability that many had taken for granted, assuming that open-source software was inherently secure simply because it was open and transparent.

The open-source community has long been celebrated for its ability to create powerful, reliable tools through collective effort. But as the XZ utils attack demonstrated, the very openness that makes these projects so valuable also leaves them susceptible to manipulation. Open-source software relies on volunteers—developers who, for the most part, are not paid for their contributions. These volunteers take on the responsibility of maintaining, updating, and improving the software, often without the resources or infrastructure needed to properly secure it. And in the case of XZ utils, this lack of support created a perfect storm for exploitation.

The attack didn't just reveal a flaw in the software itself; it highlighted the risks of relying on a system that depends on unpaid, often overburdened contributors to keep things running smoothly. Developers, even those as dedicated as Lassa Colin, can only do so much. When the demands of maintaining complex software become too great, and when there are not enough resources to properly manage and secure the project, vulnerabilities can slip through the cracks. In this case, the attacker was able to exploit a trusted, widely-used tool by infiltrating its development process—something that would have been much harder to pull off if the project had received the kind of support it needed.

But the problem goes deeper than just volunteerism. The XZ utils attack underscores a broader issue with how we think about the security of open-source projects. Many open-source tools form the backbone of modern infrastructure—powering everything from government systems to hospitals to financial networks. Yet, these projects are often maintained by individuals working in their spare time, without the financial backing or professional resources that would ensure their security. The attack on XZ utils wasn't an isolated incident; it was a cautionary tale about the risks of ignoring the vulnerabilities that exist in the open-source ecosystem.

The lesson here is clear: open-source projects cannot be left to fend for themselves. These tools are too important to be maintained by volunteers alone. There needs to be better funding, better support, and better resources to ensure that these projects are secure. Governments, corporations, and other stakeholders must recognize the critical role that open-source software plays in the functioning of the digital world, and they must step up to support these projects in a meaningful way. Without proper funding and security protocols, the open-source ecosystem will remain vulnerable to manipulation and exploitation.

In addition to funding and resources, there is a pressing need for stronger security frameworks to protect open-source projects. The XZ utils attack was a clear example of how sophisticated, targeted cyberattacks can bypass traditional security measures. These attacks rely not only on exploiting technical flaws but also on manipulating the human element—the developers who, out of necessity or convenience, fail to fully vet every line of code contributed to a project. What happened to XZ utils wasn't just a technical failure; it was a failure in the structure of how open-source projects are managed. To prevent similar incidents in the future, the cybersecurity community must advocate for stronger governance structures, more rigorous code review processes, and greater accountability for contributors.

Furthermore, this attack highlighted the need for society as a whole to build stronger cybersecurity frameworks to protect critical infrastructure. While open-source projects are a key part of the equation, they are only one piece of a much larger puzzle. The digital infrastructure of governments, businesses, hospitals, and utilities is vast and complex, and securing it requires a holistic, multi-layered approach. We need more than just reactive measures; we need proactive strategies that anticipate vulnerabilities before they are exploited. This means investing in cybersecurity at every level—from the individual developer to the largest multinational corporation—to ensure that our digital systems are resilient, secure, and able to withstand the growing threats posed by cybercriminals and state-sponsored hackers.

In the wake of the XZ utils attack, the global community must take a hard look at how it approaches cybersecurity. The attack was a reminder that the digital world is a shared responsibility, and everyone—whether they are a volunteer working on an open-source project or a government agency overseeing critical infrastructure—has a role to play in protecting it. The lessons learned from this incident must lead to actionable changes, including increased support for open-source software, improved security practices, and stronger frameworks for safeguarding the digital world. Only then will we be able to ensure that the infrastructure on which our modern society depends is truly secure and resilient in the face of evolving cyber threats.

The XZ utils attack wasn't just a close call—it was a call to action. The time to build a more secure, more sustainable digital world is now.

CHAPTER 10

A Hero in the Shadows

In the world of cybersecurity, heroes rarely wear capes or bask in the limelight. Their victories often go unnoticed, and their efforts are typically hidden behind the scenes, out of sight from the public eye. But in the case of Andres, the story was different. His quick thinking and decisive action prevented a global cyber disaster, one that could have crippled critical infrastructure and wreaked havoc on millions of systems. Despite his quiet, unassuming role in the event, Andres was nothing short of a hero—a hero who stepped in just in time to stop a catastrophe that could have shaken the very foundation of the digital world.

Andres's role in this crisis was not that of a flashy, headline-grabbing figure. He wasn't a high-profile cybersecurity expert or a well-known hacker turned hero. He was, in essence, a regular developer—doing his job, running tests, and noticing the kind of subtle anomaly that would have been overlooked by most. It was this attention to detail, this dedication to the craft, that ultimately saved the day. When he discovered the backdoor in XZ utils, he didn't hesitate. His immediate response, his instinct to dive deeper and report the issue, averted what could have been one of the largest and most devastating cyberattacks in history.

For many in the cybersecurity community, Andres's actions were a stark reminder of the critical role that every developer, every technician, and every IT professional plays in protecting the digital world. While the story of the XZ utils attack may have been dramatic in its execution, it was also a testament to the power of vigilance and the importance of paying attention to the small, seemingly insignificant details. Andres's heroic actions were the result of years of experience, knowledge, and a commitment to the craft—qualities that every developer and cybersecurity expert shares in their own right.

But it wasn't just Andres who acted heroically. In fact, his actions were part of a much larger, often unseen network of professionals who work tirelessly to protect the digital infrastructure that we all rely on. The unsung heroes of cybersecurity are the everyday developers, the volunteer contributors to open-source projects, and the security experts who fight against the growing tide of cyber threats. These individuals often work in the shadows, without recognition, and with little fanfare. Yet, it is their collective effort that keeps the digital world secure.

Cybersecurity is a vast, complex field that involves not just high-profile experts in government or large corporations but also a diverse group of individuals who play an integral role in maintaining the security of our systems. From developers working on open-source projects to system administrators monitoring server traffic, these everyday heroes are the ones who ensure that our personal data, our communications, and our businesses remain safe from those who would exploit the system for malicious gain.

The XZ utils attack was just one example of the ever-present danger that lurks in the digital world. Every day, cybersecurity professionals around the world work to prevent breaches, detect vulnerabilities, and respond to the constant threat of cybercrime. Their work often goes unnoticed by the public, but it is their tireless efforts that keep the systems we take for granted secure and functioning. These unsung heroes are the backbone of the digital age, and without them, the digital world would be a much more dangerous place.

The future of cybersecurity, as highlighted by the XZ utils attack, must be one of vigilance, collaboration, and preparedness. The attack exposed the vulnerabilities that exist in the open-source ecosystem, but it also showed the resilience and strength of the cybersecurity community. The world learned valuable lessons from this close call: how important it is to support open-source projects, how essential it is to vet every line of code, and how easily even the most trusted systems can be compromised.

But as we look to the future, it's clear that the threat landscape is constantly evolving. Cybercriminals and state-sponsored attackers are becoming increasingly sophisticated, and the digital infrastructure we rely on is only growing more complex. The next digital time bomb could be just around the corner, and the cybersecurity community must be prepared for whatever comes next.

To prepare for the next attack, the world must learn to adapt. We must strengthen the frameworks that govern the security of open-source projects, invest in better resources and support for the developers who maintain them, and build more robust systems to detect and neutralize threats before they can cause harm. More importantly, we must continue to foster a culture of collaboration and vigilance, where every developer, every security expert, and every user plays an active role in protecting the digital world.

The future of cybersecurity is not just about preventing the next big attack—it's about creating an ecosystem where security is built into the foundation of every system, where collaboration is the norm, and where heroes like Andres are supported by the global community to continue their vital work. As we move forward, we must remember that the fight against cyber threats is ongoing, and that the heroes of tomorrow will continue to work in the shadows, ensuring that the digital world remains secure for everyone.

In the end, Andres's story serves as both a cautionary tale and a beacon of hope. A reminder that the digital world is vulnerable, but also a testament to the power of vigilance, collaboration, and the unsung heroes who make the internet a safer place for us all.

CONCLUSION

In the rush of everyday life, we often take for granted the convenience and connectivity that the digital world provides. We rely on it for nearly every aspect of our existence— communication, banking, healthcare, and even governance. But beneath the surface of this vast, interconnected world lies a quiet, often invisible danger. The attack on XZ utils served as a sobering reminder of how vulnerable our digital systems really are. What might seem like a harmless bug or a routine glitch can, in reality, be the precursor to a catastrophic event that threatens the integrity of our most vital systems.

The digital age has brought incredible benefits, but it has also introduced a new set of risks. As we become more reliant on digital infrastructure, the consequences of a single breach grow exponentially. The XZ utils backdoor was hidden within one of the most trusted open-source tools in the world— something that millions of servers depend on daily. Yet, for all its familiarity and utility, it contained a vulnerability so subtle and well-concealed that even the most experienced developers failed to spot it. This silent threat could have spread like wildfire, compromising critical systems and exposing sensitive data on a global scale.

What's perhaps most unsettling is that the XZ utils attack was not an isolated incident. It was a wake-up call to the many threats that exist within our digital infrastructure, threats that are often difficult to detect and even harder to defend against. The attackers didn't rely solely on technical skill; they also understood human behavior, exploiting the collaborative nature of open-source development to insert their malicious code undetected. The digital world is more interconnected than ever before, and with that connection comes greater vulnerability.

As we reflect on these vulnerabilities, one thing becomes abundantly clear: the importance of vigilance cannot be overstated. The fight against cyber threats is not one that can be left to the experts alone. It requires a collective effort, with every developer, every security expert, and even every user playing a role in keeping the internet safe. Andres's discovery was a perfect example of how one individual's vigilance made all the difference. His keen eye caught a subtle anomaly, which, when followed to its logical conclusion, revealed a massive vulnerability. Had he ignored the red flags, the results could have been disastrous.

This attack also underscores the necessity of strengthening our collective cybersecurity efforts. It's not just about having sophisticated tools or strong firewalls in place—it's about creating a culture of awareness, where everyone involved in digital development and usage understands the potential risks and acts accordingly. The cybersecurity community, the open-source community, and the digital infrastructure at large must work together to build systems that are not only functional but also resilient against the ever-evolving landscape of threats.

Andres's actions, though heroic, should not stand as the exception but the rule. His discovery, the subsequent fallout, and the changes that followed in cybersecurity protocols all highlight the pressing need for better safeguards, better communication, and better systems. Since the XZ utils attack, cybersecurity practices have evolved, and organizations have become more proactive in seeking out vulnerabilities and addressing them before they can be exploited. The world has learned that relying on open-source software, while powerful, requires ongoing diligence and resources to ensure its security.

In the aftermath of the attack, the digital world began to adopt stricter guidelines for open-source contributions, improved vetting procedures, and stronger security measures. The response was swift, but it also revealed just how much more needs to be done. The lasting impact of Andres's discovery is not just the prevention of a global disaster—it is the awareness it sparked in the cybersecurity community and beyond. It forced us to acknowledge that the digital world is fragile, and that we must be ever watchful to protect the systems that sustain modern life.

As we move forward, we must remain vigilant, understanding that the next attack could be just as subtle and just as dangerous. The lessons learned from the XZ utils attack are ones that should shape our approach to cybersecurity for years to come. The digital world will continue to evolve, but with better safeguards, more collaboration, and an ever-growing commitment to vigilance, we can build a more secure and resilient future for all.